Women Who Dye
Their Hair

Acknowledgements
Thanks are due to the editors of the following publications
in which some of these poems have appeared:
*Atlantic Review, Blade, Brando's Hat, Hanging Loose, The
Interpreter's House, Overdraft, P.N. Review, The Rialto,
Scratch, Sheaf, Smiths Knoll, Soup Dragon, The Wide Skirt.*

Women Who Dye
Their Hair

Janet Fisher

Smith/Doorstop Books

Published 2001 by
Smith/Doorstop Books
The Poetry Business
The Studio
Byram Arcade
Westgate
Huddersfield HD1 1ND

ISBN 1-902382-25-0

British Library Cataloguing-in-Publication Data. A catalogue
record for this book is available from the British Library.

Typeset at The Poetry Business
Printed by Peepal Tree, Leeds

Cover picture: 'Three Women', by Fernand Leger

Smith/Doorstop are represented by Signature Books, 2 Little Peter
Street, Manchester M15 4PS, and distributed by Littlehampton
Book Services Ltd.

The Poetry Business gratefully acknowledges the help of Kirklees
Metropolitan Council and Yorkshire Arts.

CONTENTS

7	Women Who Dye Their Hair
8	Autobiography of a Careless Woman
9	The Very Happy
10	I'm No Longer Ever Likely
11	Just the Facts
12	We Are So Close
13	Storm
14	Different Versions
15	Christmas Present
16	Early Retirement
17	And So On
18	The Price of Fame
19	Workshop
20	Raking the Moon
21	The Plot Keeps Changing
22	The Day Ted Hughes Died
23	31.8.97
24	Net Working
25	Natural Wastage
26	Party
27	Thanks
28	How It Was
29	Last Days
30	The New China
34	Treasure Island
35	The Organ Blower
36	Radio Waves
37	Strangers on the Shore
38	Benedicite, Omnia Opera
40	Chipping Norton
41	A Dream of Fennel
42	The Quilter
43	The Gardener
44	To Pain

45	Rigor
46	Knee Job
47	Tunnel Vision
48	Family Ghosts
49	Red Eye
50	C.W.G.
52	House For Sale. No Chain.
53	Turning Out The House
54	Lilies
55	Doors
56	Mother's Day
57	Fish
58	The Festival Called Holi
59	The Red Road
60	'Griff'
61	Time
62	Patience
63	Gap Year
64	Raspberry Jam
65	Tin Roofs
66	On Roosevelt Island.
67	Once
68	She Thought She'd Found God

Women Who Dye Their Hair

Some of us have done it since our twenties
when our hair turned white on the death of a loved one
or it ran in the family like baldness, and some of us
spray red or purple on shaved stubble,
and others have let it creep up on us,
counting the odd hair, then the fifth, the fiftieth,
till our teenagers point out how old we're getting
but our lovers who hate anything artificial
like make-up and sequins, though they accept
icecream and the Pill, say we shouldn't bother,
so we steal home from Boots with the ColorGlo
and lock ourselves in the bathroom in rubber gloves,
emerge an hour later ten years younger
with a smart grey streak over one temple
and mahogany smudges round the jaw line.
And when the roots start to show we carelessly
pop into the hairdresser and book a colour
which means a cut and finish and takes all morning
so we can catch up on our reading, extending
our knowledge of the stars and multiple orgasm,
but we have to go every six weeks or it starts to fade
and by now the local firm is turning our hair to hay
so we find a better one at fifty quid a splash,
a rollercoaster we can't get off of,
and we decide to let it all grow out and be our age
which isn't a hundred and five but might as well be.

Autobiography of a Careless Woman

You see now how I've ambled down the years,
drawn no conclusions, left no alibis,
done good and bad in roughly equal measure,
avoided pain, but not won many prizes
for best behaviour, and I can't devise
the way things happen – life comes as it will,
perched on my shoulder, pecking at my ear.
I gamble my intentions on a quick thrill,
working the odds, prepared to pay the price,
but giving more than I had bargained for,
parade my virtue and conceal my vice,
relishing both and going for the double.
Too much commitment only brings you trouble;
as mother says, it's bound to end in tears
but at the moment things are very nice.

The Very Happy

always have kind grins
when they catch themselves in the mirror
running their fingers through their hair.
Nothing is too much trouble. Though
they've planned to spend the day sunbathing,
when they sense you need to talk
they'll listen seriously, offer good advice,
the sort they'll never need themselves.
If you break a leg they say how lucky
it wasn't your neck, and if you break your neck
they teach you to paint with your teeth.

I'm No Longer Ever Likely

to stride across muddy fields at daybreak
against a red sky, a nip of frost, towards
tea, a bacon sandwich and no questions,

or dance salsa in high heels, hip
and toe on the beat, perfect,
swirling my red skirt over a foam of petticoats,

or slip at midnight aboard the cargo boat,
hat slouched, eye on the tides and the flash
of searchlights through the fog.

Will these do instead: a hand at my elbow,
cloud shadows skirting a carpet of crocuses,
an anchor sinking into the river's soft bed?

Just the Facts

Swallows are not dropped stitches
in the newly knitted morning,
nor notes on a stave of wires.

It's Wednesday, 5 pm, November.
A flask of tea and fruitcake
on a damp bench.

The stars are dropped stitches
in the cloth of twilight.

We Are So Close

your hair springs like wire from my tight scalp,
my armpits sticky with your sweat,
your flatulence ripping my guts.

Your nerves string my spine, my body tensile –
hang me upside down, I'll sway in the wind,
keep my balance when you drag me upright.

Your blood sluices my heart,
your marrow lines my inaccessible bones,
my flesh sealed with your skin.

I carry your nightmares in my head,
your voices pierce my throat,
I brush your dirt from my fingernails,
search for your future in my palm.

Storm

It's as if it were meant,
our coming together, not
in the doubletalk of a crude joke
but the way lightning and thunder
break through the sky, their separation
a time-lapsed spasmodic affair
like our letters a month apart,
phone calls squeezed in,
till at last, hands gingerly linked
on the bus and the short run
through the first heavy spots
to your room, we stand
for a moment at the window
as the heavens open.

Different Versions

Some things he can't bear
to throw out: his Bush radio,
the Decca gramophone saved for
from his grant. Neither work.

And now good decks are hard
to come by, his records stack
useless in the cupboard he had built,
their cellophane skins cracked and dusty.

Guilini, Barbirolli: they roll off the tongue.
Hans Schmidt-Isserstedt. Horns,
scrolls, dim photos of orchestras.
The day Queens Park got relegated

he played me *Kindertotenlieder*
as we lay on his narrow bed.
He never put on the records I bought him
because I liked the sleeve or the name –

I didn't know then that Menuhin's
Beethoven verged on the sentimental,
that he preferred, as I do now, Suk or Oistrakh,
a precision that cuts to the quick.

Christmas Present

We sat up late over a few old movies so
we were just a bit hung over when we kissed
goodbye at lunchtime and their old gate set
in a hard stone wall slammed shut in a gust,
slicing through the top of my finger.
They'd barely basted the roast when we rushed back
yelling but Joan who'd been on ARP knew
what to do and held my hand up declaring
the blood would stop in fifteen seconds.

An hour later I'm on my way to A&E,
Ray driving through the rain on a slipping
clutch, me with my hand still in the air.
The nurses have seen it before; I'm sent home
with four soluble sutures, three injections,
two x-rays and instructions to keep it dry
and come back Wednesday. That night
I fish out my sawn-off wedding ring
from the brown envelope and stare at it.

Early Retirement

Stumbling to the loo at six I meet you
on the landing fully dressed. Forgive me,
bemused by sleep and a dream of sleep
I hadn't noticed your empty side, so used
to your being there I didn't miss you.
You're always last to bed anyway,
dozing in front of the telly or tapping in
your new CV, but this is ridiculous,
standing there still in shirtsleeves, trying
to engage me in conversation.
Is this what it does to you?
Perhaps the video was on the blink again
so you settled in for a nap, let your late tea
go cold in front of the Learning Zone.
It's not over yet, my dear.
Dawn may be cracking beyond next door's
new up-and-over that blocks our light,
but if we don't start to talk, just snuggle
back into the wrap of sleep, though we're still
washing hands, switching off lights,
we might catch another forty winks
which will see us through past 'Today',
even into 'Woman's Hour', because
there's nothing now to get up for
except ourselves.

And So On

Tomorrow I'll be innocent
like a cat licking between its toes.
I'll imagine with pleasure
the book I'm returning to, the bottle of wine,
the film we're going to see
with a good plot and an Oscar nomination.

When he strokes a cat he talks to it
constantly, as if expecting an answer,
offers it emotions and obligations
it trembles on the edge of response to
in a twist of a furry neck,
the push of a claw.

Each day we remake each other,
see ourselves in new lights,
brush up old habits, treating the long course
of our life together like the three peaks race,
turning our ankles on rocky outcrops,
dazzled by the sun glancing off windows.

I mould my days, firm them up
in my fingers, give them away as presents.
No more sloppiness: up by seven
putting the washing on, writing lists,
hearing nothing but the thud of my own voice
against the wall of my brain.

The Price of Fame

My mug with your face on plays jingle bells
as I drink to your T-shirt. The Council
upload a blue plaque to your web site.
I open a paper, turn on the radio: it's you again;
I look up, you fly by, waving.

I take the deep steps to the shoreline;
far off voices shift, thin out, but yours
is in my head, your smile on my currency,
your name trailed in vapour, spelt out in flowers,
stamped on a star at my feet.

Workshop

Late as always, walking in with a bag of leeks
and poems, a guest at her own wedding,
having trawled the market for spices
and the last tomatoes. They clap,
full of their own conversations, never mind
excuses: the broken lift, the pickle jar,
the cardiac arrest. Hello and goodbye is not
what they want to hear, they've paid for this,
the hollow-stomach-ness, the when-did-you-
last-see-your-father-ness, the flash
like a pigeon crossing the overhead cable.

Raking the Moon

It smiles up at us. Our rakes balance
muscular arms, foreshortened legs:

the perspective's not good. Shadows
cut sharp across the bridge.
Why do we want it so, this madness –
a rich source of calcium, home for strange men,

origin of dreams. What a prize
to have on the mantelpiece:
strangers arriving to bask in its pale light,
cool their hands on its glow.

We haunt the canal edge,
feel our way perilously round the weeds.
The old woman in her nightie leans
from the upstairs, poised at an unlikely angle.

'What is the meaning of this!' she shouts,
and we scratch our heads.

The Plot Keeps Changing

2 am, I'm not listening to my heart beat
or designing cushions or next year's meals
in the new oven I haven't got the hang of yet.
Sandalwood and jasmine by the bed take me
down beyond the real to the really real,
putting off the everyday, its brass tacks quiddity:

next day I check the spelling, leafing through,
with a magnifying glass that catches the light,
bars me from the ninety six meanings of 'natural',
then I scour the thesaurus, rip out pages,
my black pen ringing the words that sound good,
till the blank sheet's ready for my words: stumbling,
unalphabetical, deranged, pockmarked, out of order,
out of place, off the record and leading nowhere.

The Day Ted Hughes Died

John Glenn's packing, ready to beat
the clock again. He reaches to the back
of the wardrobe, unzips the plastic,
brushes off a spider.
It still fits!

He spreads his shoulders,
remembers the speeches, the flames,
faces like upturned small moons. The fear.
It's all out there through the layers of air:
sucking up New York steak, crapping
into a vacuum pack, bumping his head
on the cabin roof (gee, this is fun!).

For years he's lain awake, hooked,
snaking through an owl-ridden dark
into the heavens, envious, needing
to be there. No one knows.
And now it's all to go again, he's fit,
flexing muscle, proving he's still got it,
what it takes.

But what if the bearings
were out by a sliver,
the ship wrongly aligned,
he'd swing on and away
beyond everything,
past the Great Bear,
the Hunter, the Dog Star,
Fishes, Bull,
seeing them always and finally
for what they are.

31.8.97

Midnight, the water won't go away,
sicks itself back: a blockage
far down the pipe, out of reach
of plunger or coat hanger. The radio dishes
the Saturday latest. Who won what.
Perhaps it's a bleach job, or caustic
to skin my fingers, bring on my asthma,
fail. 'Sailing By' and the Shipping.
But the World Service breaks the news,
and I poke and plunge, gloved now
and masked, to free the backed up gunge.
No good. Next day it's still there, worse.
I ladle the scum into buckets;
it's pissing down, drone, drone:
who knew her, who loved her, plumbers
who won't turn out on a Sunday, and flowers
banked up enough for an avalanche.
It's a holiday – no cooking, no telly –
so we eat out, drive to Homebase,
Du Pré's Elgar riding the storm,
for a stronger plunger. Pointless.

Late Monday the plumber shows,
saws a new trap door, drops under
to unstuff the elbow, get us running clear.

Net Working

I've discovered BT PhoneNetUK.
Cheaper, more casual, than 192,
you can browse the country
for the price of a call.
Key in the names of ex-lovers,
guess the areas they might be living in
(it's easier if they have unusual names:
Lillywhite, Wellbeloved, Latimer-Sayer).
It gives the address as well.

There's another site with maps:
enter the postcode and you're there.
You can survey the district, home in large,
pinpoint the street, the house.
Find an estate agent,
book an online rental
in a room opposite.
Set up the webcam.

Natural Wastage

Elaine points to cats as proof that God exists.
From West Nab *the world feels like a pebble
in the hand of Jesus*; shaky ground but she trudges on.
Even the Big Bang had to start somewhere.

Frank thinks the universe is circular. *On and on.*

Black holes are by their nature provocative,
unclaimable, good as metaphor.
A transferrable power of minus infinity
says Frank, hooked on space games.

Walking on tussocks is like walking on cats.

Wiping the peat from our boots we drive back
for egg and chips. Frank reads out the funny bits,
the headlines claim another thousand dead,
and she carries on about the circulation of the blood.

Party

In lit rooms of early evening, guests pose
at windows, balance glass and cigarette,
fake smiles of recognition or dalliance.
How love transfixes us. I am pressed
to a crisp by a man in a fawn jacket

and when his eyes meet mine
it's a stab in the dark. ('What's that mark
on your dress, dear?' 'It's only wine,
some idiot jogged my arm.')

I hear outside voices, the slam
of a door. Beyond the turn of the hedge
the sunset is knifed onto a reluctant sky;
under the hillocks sugaring the lawn
the moles are at their eternal tunnelling.

Thanks

Thanks for the poem.
I really like it.
Did you write it specially?

Thanks for the poem.
How long did it take to write?
Did the trees change colour as you wrote it?
Did the swallows leave home?

Thanks for the poem.
Don't apologise.
We all got the point.

Thanks for the poem.
Where do you get your ideas from?

Thanks for the poem.
It's very clever I suppose,
just don't show it to your father.

Thanks for the poem.
I've made some suggestions,
just a few. I'll fax them over
but don't worry,
I really like it.

How It Was

The flood was up
but it's over now, sunk down
below the mark on the bridge:
this is where we were then,
my bonnet trailing by its ribbon
on the cinder track, my boots
up to their buttons in mud.

Now old men pass me with dogs,
cigarettes hid in their palms,
and on the canal an icebreaker,
somebody's home, radio
hung on the rail, no longer
cutting a path for the coal barges
on a bitter morning.

The last train pushed on past us;
the steam blew a speck in my eye.
The fog comes down, real this time,
and I'm glad of the fencing
to keep me from the water.
You need straight lines in the fog.
I stumble, grab at the catkins

and the green of them
stains my glove and my finger
through the hole I haven't darned yet.
The paper I find thrust in my pocket
has your writing on it, hurried,
crosshatched as if paper were short,
which it might be where you come from.

Last Days

I was pretty then. He called me his monkey,
fondled my neck. On feast days I wore cloth of gold,
my hair braided with amethyst. He kissed my throat
and I trembled. This was enchantment:
figures half seen in the rose garden,
a flag flying from the battlements.

Now this lump crouches inside me.
My chamberlain brings me soup and bread,
urges me to eat, but I'm greedy for delicacies:
fondants and marzipan. I look in the glass
at my puffy face, and laugh. When the child kicks
I strike back with my thick fist, there and there.
How can such a thing be born?

I hear my lord has gone to the war.
He writes me heroic poems
and I don't read them. I drink some wine.
It turns my head and I have to lie down.
I was a virgin and now I am this.

I think they'll take the child from me,
drown me as a witch, throw my lovely dresses
on the fire, and all my books. But
they don't know the measure of it,
the power I had and lost. I pray to the Virgin
and she turns her head away and simpers.

In a dream he comes to me in my closet,
skin like brocade, shadows staining his eyes,
through my window open to the evening star
fixed for one moment in the turning sky,
a flicker of eternity, like a rabbit's scut
skidding down a burrow across dead fields
washed and laid out under the moon.

The New China

Kindergarten
They are fluent in English.
'Hallo. My name is Hannah. I am four.'
Open or shy, they grab attention,
show us their work.
They're only children.

The playground is painted
with Disney folk,
wide-eyed and soupy.
There's a line on the ground
which they march along, singing.

Outside, street traders
push rayon dressed as silk,
glass jade.

Bird and Flower Market, Shanghai
The old man sits on a stool
scooping in noodles, watching me,
his narrow stall a jungle
of maple and magnolia;
at his feet bowls of bulbous guppies,
crickets and kittens in cages,
baby turtles scrambling for air.

I can't speak his language.
I smile, poke a finger through the wire,
and he taps out a price on his calculator,
hands it to me to bargain, but I hold back,
embarrassed I don't know
what's for eating
what's for company.

Amenities
The first two spots have English menus
but not English loos. They plead with me to stay,
offer me a stool, arms to hang from,
but pride and arthritis drive me out.

Suzhou
Cobblers on a street corner
cutting new heels
for a young woman in blue.

Sechuan Hot Pot
The café is clean, crowded,
not a whisper, a scribble, of English.
Steaming pots inset in tables,
gas burners by our knees,
are divided yin-yang style
into white tasty and red hot.
A duck's head bobs.
We drop in eel, pork, cuttlefish
til they're cooked and crunchy.

Beer and Coke are on the house.
Six waiters teach us what to do;
by the time the sliced fruit comes
we're all in stitches.

Traffic
Bikes, scooters, taxis, pickups,
swoop and weave
in vast communal trust.

At the North Temple Pagoda tea room
A business man
talks non-stop into a mobile,
lights a cigarette,
talks non-stop to his companion,
hawks and spits.

I drink green tea
from a mug with blue dragons,
a flask of hot water to top up.

Through a loudspeaker
a passing Japanese
controls his group.

Wumen Bridge
Over the canal to Pan Man Gate,
the old city defences,
we run the gauntlet of traders:
Little Red Books, sweat-stained,
carvings, antiques,
cheap plates too risky
to carry home without breaking.

Rain in Xiling Gorge
We crowd into the Lotus bar,
peer upstream.
The guide holds up a book of photos,
shows us what we're looking at.

Chongqing
Her English is better than expected
but we still speak slowly.
She points out the caves they used
as shelters from Japanese bombs,
now stores and garages.
The taxi winds up through the damp,
pollution worsening our coughs.
I say it's just like Seattle.
She's delighted:
'Our twin city!'

Flying Home Over Mongolia
Thirty thousand feet below us
a woman in a yurt
stuffed with family and animals
is stewing up the bits from a yak
you can't sell, wear or sleep on.

Treasure Island

She reads aloud to us, her voice sharp;
her clever fingers pattern the desk.
The smell of dinner smothers the wallflowers.

Last week at hometime he knelt over me,
bruised his fists into my face,
thighs, elbows, gritty with tarmac.

Her voice is sharp, they call her Miss Mustard,
I am her pet. I get good reports.
The bees flatter the velvet wallflowers;
their claret and mustard spoil in the heat.

Last night they dragged me under a bush,
the sky dull gold like the wheatfields.

Her voice is sharp, her stories entrancing,
Miss Mustard smells as sweet as soap.
Blind Pew taps his stick, hands out the black spot.

The days spread their gold
like wheatfields at sunset, a dull sky
white and gold like the wallflowers.

Each day I wake to a fickle world
a step nearer to the ending of it,
each day an infringement, a dull wind
blowing in from the wheatfields.

Miss Mustard reads, her voice disarming,
her clever fingers plait the milk straws.

I am Jim the cabin boy in a barrel of apples;
the flowers smell sweeter as the sun strengthens.

The Organic Blower

His cheerful face bobs
up and down through the curtains.
Harvest Sunday, chapel full, sills
piled with onions. The walls
are chalky pastel, like love hearts.

I drag home behind my mother
in her good hat with the brim
the Sunday School girls
like to drop bits in. I'm sobbing
but can't explain. Next night

is the auction: sprigs of grapes,
windfalls, cottage loaves – the tops
pull off like plaster, insides
soft as a wound. Afterwards
the concert: Derek on musical saw
cradled between his knees.

Twenty years on, in the pub
he grasps my hand, spluttering.
Can't read or write, calculates
back from 501, infallible.

Radio Waves

My Saturday jobs are to salt the slugs
and carry the accumulators up the road
to Beardsleys for a refill, so we can hear
Workers' Playtime, Children's Hour, Journey

Into Space. Bakelite, back lit in gold,
hissing voices tracked by a finger,
a slit in the fabric. I'm in there.
The shiny oil lamp reflects the firelight.

On fine days hens wander indoors, dump
slippy whorls on the tiles, their eggs ditched
in hedges or behind the coal hole.
Some go broody, and that's forbidden:

eggs are for eating, chicks are collected
from the station, a day old, a dozen to the box,
Easter fluff soon lost in pullet gawk,
they bully and peck, eyes dotty with hate.

*

Hot June nights I lie in my baby-dolls,
bonfire smoke in my eyes, up my nose,
tuned to 208: Buddy and Elvis, Platters
saving the last dance for me.

*

The bed's hard, the nurses noisy,
the wound aches. I plug in to massacres,
broken talks, a flood. The World Service's
the only thing that keeps me asleep.

Strangers on the Shore

1.
White smile creased to a turn, he serves cheese
to village women in lisle and headscarves,
sit-up-and-beg bikes pedal down on the curb.

It isn't in question: the war, escape, the journey
through to career, daughters, diabetes; and now he's here,
unorthodox certainly, hats off to them,

they wouldn't stomach a yarmulke. But it's not enough.
Talk dies down as he struggles with the bacon slicer.
The thing of it is, he needs – not acceptance exactly –

identity, the stamp of it on what he sells, what he recovers
from the people who when he shakes their hands
and smiles, do it back at him, loving it.

2.
I stacked his shelves for £3 a week,
the summer between school and university.
New fittings were built by the local joiner
who date stamped my forehead in his dinner hour,

took me down the Nissen hut rifle range,
steadied the butt against my shoulder,
helped me squeeze as I scored two bull's-eyes,
the nicotine on his breath drying my mouth.

Benedicite, Omnia Opera

A landmark, it sat square by the pub and bus stop,
a hundred feet high, dark slabs of ironstone
and a three faced clock wound up each Monday
by the sweating verger. The banging bells made us
who lived under them bang our heads on practice nights

and twice on Sundays, and New Year's Eve, the muffs on,
then off at midnight, ding donging us into resolution.
The graves were thick with lichen through the leggy grasses.
I went to Communion at eight each Sunday,
even before a cup of tea. Anglicanism at its purest,

congregation quiet at the side altar, the vicar mumbling;
Mr Bletsoe taking the collection
counted heads out loud: they didn't want
to bless too many portions of bread and wine.
The wafer melting on my tongue was sweet

like sherbert flying saucers, two a penny
from the baths café where we spent our Saturdays
in frilly bathing suits and rubber hats.
The wine was like the port my father's boss
watered for me on Christmas duty lunches:

cold lamb and warm icecream over jelly
followed by halma and, if lucky, Scrabble.
I liked better the noisy nights at aunty Joyce's,
first sips of whisky macs or cherry brandy,
chancing pennies on pontoon and Chase-the-Ace.

Each cold Good Friday from twelve till three
the church was darkened into meditation,
the Lenten litanies on the home straight,
the altar bare, waiting on Easter lilies.
I'd go to the bakers early with half a crown

then Mum and I walked the fields to hear the larks
pitching into the blue. These ancient ceremonies
drew me in; I could almost believe in salvation.
Rock'n'roll and resurrection, ice in the wind.
All ye works of the Lord, bless ye the Lord.

Some things I long for, some I'm not very good at.
Those cool Saturdays queuing for the high board,
chlorine-wrinkled skin and the first shivers of summer.

Chipping Norton

The danger is wanting to stay forever.
Our last night, weather blown over,
heavy on cider and wine we make clues
with each other's names. *Shorn link – an ache.*
Tomorrow the circle breaks,
O marshy friend, house returned,
beds remade, kitchen emptied
of our food, our laughter.
Him sham, as of jester.

No more words: we are full, ripened
like greenhouse tomatoes, ready for autumn.
Nightcaps on. *If she ran – jet!*
The cricket scores will have to wait
for the morning papers. *Lid or anvil?*
I smell the cigars on his breath, follow him
into the garden for one last puff.

A Dream of Fennel

for Rachel/Margaret

The tree you gave me when we reached fifty,
the fossil tree, that survived Hiroshima,
grows slow and strong each spring;
its alien leaves push from the nodes
in its stubby trunk. Extract of ginko:
good for clear thinking and memory.

*

I'm spilled light-headed into oblivion
by my therapist's fingers treading
muscle and tendon, digging into weak spots:
I'm stretching to reach giant seedcases
of ridged fennel, sticky with aniseed.
The oil, she says, is for swellings and hormones.

From the deep woods her house overlooks,
baby jackdaws cry out for food
against a waterfall of hawthorn.

*

Some photos showed up last week:
of us at twelve in my house, arms and legs
at all angles, pulling scary grins;
you at your New York wedding in stiff lace;
the one of your girls at five? eight? the younger
squeezing her sister's face.

                                    I'll ring soon:

I've dug a new border, planted fennel
in the sun; its purple-green leaves feathered
like lungs grow taller than any of us.

The Quilter

for Sue

Inbetween shop and family, stacking,
digging and laying, buying in and seeing off,
a twentyfour/seven way of life, you find
space in your spare room, a bag of bits,
setting a green against a blue or red
well pieced and bordered, the backing
neat as the top we're meant to look at.

You seed your natural world onto calico,
linen or cambric, nothing too tough for a needle.
Patchwork, appliqué, whole cloth, they carpet
your walls in multitudes, corner your visitors.
Some are samplers but most are the real thing,
layers of tone and texture, deep-rooted,
that win prizes, but can't or won't be sold.

The Gardener

In apron and anorak he beds the soil
to the lawn's edge, perks up
a nameless shoot, gives it its spot
like a teacher with a shy infant.

With backpack and hose
he glides round the paths,
a moon man
silvering the moss,
knowing what's best.

Each hour he gives is worth two,
but when I pay him from the kitchen door
in my dressing gown, on my third coffee,
the green solitude that's embraced him all morning
spills into talk, of his finds, plans, assumptions.

I poke the hoe round the shorn lavender,
holding my breath, like a working mother
on the minder's day off.

To Pain

You're fond of games, you play hide and seek,
hang about in the wardrobe, under the bath,
peekaboo through your fingers, just for a laugh.
I count to a hundred, don't move, hold my breath.

Catch as catch can, you tease me, your shadow
nipping down alleyways, peeping through windows,
at my back or beside me; sometimes it's cast
right up in front of me, won't let me past.

You grip hand, leg, the nape of my neck,
no holds barred, you tighten the armlock,
living my life for me, pinning me down,
my common law lover, my toy boy, my clown.

I'd dull you with drugs, pack you off home,
you'd sulk by the telephone, sucking your thumb.
I'd give you the finger, tell the tale on you,
stick my stamp on you, sack you and mail you:

but you'd say I'm a coward, you'd think I can't hack it.
And what it boils down to is how do I see you:
a face in my mirror, a head on my pillow,
or a gun in the ribs and your hand in my pocket.

Rigor

The mercury's shot up past danger
and I'm perishing, so hot I'm cold,
trembling like a charismatic –
I want to bury myself
under blankets with hot water bottles
but I'm laid on a sheet
windows wide, fan on, till the fever's
washed across me, damp seaweed
drowning in air, bones light as membrane,
flushes shapeshifting over my skin.

Knee Job

All I want is to walk quickly,
to browse or go window shopping,
ignore the cracks in the pavement,
not bothering what people think,
strangers holding the door,
telling me about brave brothers
climbing Snowdon now and riding bikes.

At sixteen I spent a fortnight in hospital,
a dummy in a long row of dummies,
food dished out from steaming saucepans,
bowels monitored every morning,
and on the other side of the ward
a woman I'd hardly got to know
was laid out behind screens.

It's a wonder I'm still alive.

I dream I'm in front of the crowd,
knowing what they're after.
I wake up and they're still shouting:
'We tried to tell you how serious it was,'
and I shout back:
'What do you think I have
that I don't know about?'

In a high tech world I'm barefoot,
padding a path across ricefields
with out-of-date medicines, boiled needles.
I can make a tourniquet from tights,
a splint from a chair leg.
Five scalpels hang on the kitchen wall
and the stretcher is the plank I stand on.

Tunnel Vision

A chart to read double length from a mirror
through iron frames a Tudor lord might wear,
or an alchemist. A lens turning at a finger's click
to optimise the red or green, the zigzag.
Then a popgun firing air at an eyeball,
gauging the pressure, the warning signal.

Don't blink. Next, forehead on a plastic bar,
a button to press each time I see a light,
pinpoint the quick movement of the stars.
'Have you noticed any deterioration of sight?'
They dazzle me with instruments. The surgery
turns black, an after image, compensatory.

Twice a day I pull my lower lid,
expose the watery pink, flinch at the dropper.
The stuff stings. It's supposed to do me good.
My eye's distorted; it may be glaucoma.
A technicality. Two drops a day
will stop it in its tracks, or so they say.

What have I got to lose?
A wider point of view. Nuances
of recognition. The sidelong glance.
A sudden move in the shadows,
a curtain's flick. A different vision.
Life will be straightforward from now on.

Family Ghosts

Not the sort that weather themselves round you,
stream past the window shouting at owls, stand
in pools in your garden waving their severed heads
at the moon with your grandmother's hat on

but the letter you thought you hadn't received,
your undownloaded email, an over-breath,
a dried dab of blood on a bandage, or a hand
by your rib cage, back door opening at a gust.

Red Eye

Thank God we went when we did, nothing planned,
three weeks after Tom was born, carry cot crammed
in the back end of the Renault 4, his brothers
squabbling over whose space the other was in.

On the Monday we drive out, park on the disused railway,
pick early blackberries, Tom in a shawl on the grass,
while mum makes tea back at the house. Before bed
I take them down the flaking steps to the cellar

where dad keeps his musty wines, undrinkable records
of afternoons on roadsides, fingers black with dandelions.
In the corner's a pool, with frogs no one knows where from.
The boys' hands cast shadows round the dry rot.

As we leave she asks us to pose
for a last shot to use up the film.
By the kitchen window jammed with rust
the four of us are standing grinning.

C.W.G.

'*But in you is the presence that
will be, when all the stars are dead.*'
                    Rilke, 'Buddha in Glory'

Angrily through a blur of cataracts
his fingers fumble for Ribena,
the panic button. His mind is clear,
made up. His voice cracks.

The guest house, handy for the hospital,
overlooks the war memorial;
my clothes on the twin bed by the radiator
and the doorstop in the shape of a reindeer.

Before his fall he lived by himself,
did his own cooking. Moved slowly.
An hour for breakfast. An hour and a half
to bathe and dress. Shaved from memory.

I lie cramped up with stomach ache
and bad comedians, too weak
to switch off. Something I've eaten.
At 3 am I rush for the basin.

He gives me orders about the bills, tries
to pull out the catheter. I read him the headlines
from the Telegraph. 'Cheats, waste, lies.
How do they manage to keep clean?'

The certificate says bronchial pneumonia
('the old man's friend'), kidney failure.
Three days later a short cremation,
no hymns, a selection from *Patience*.

It's the funny thing about absence:
him not being there, the lack of the chance
not to be with him. I don't want to break,
but when I do it helps. Like being sick.

House For Sale. No Chain.

Maundy Thursday, I'm waiting to complete;
should I let them in anyway – they won't want
to hang around all Easter, hammers on hold.
I've emptied the cupboards, stood
shivering in the cellar looking up:
'that floor won't last.' Why not just
give them the key, forget it, let them
knock out the fireplace I always wanted
to see behind, put in new timbers, a bathroom.

The garden's large, bits sold off
over the years, like a body losing
its faculties – joints, ears, eyes, finally
the heart. It stretches south towards
the bindweed's galleries and caves
curving round the apple trees.
It's surprising to discover
how warm it is outside,
and to smell the rain.

Turning Out The House

It needs a bomb under it.
Like an archaeologist, he sifts into boxes
what's to chuck or keep, stuff to log later
layered on the piano. His hands are black:
it's a long way down.

A chocolate box, its ribbon faded: collar studs,
a lock of hair, a tooth. A signature
on a rubber stamp, ink ten years dried.
Letters from landladies, school books,
his writing no better then than now.

He checks the flowers, chats up the faces,
inexplicably lined, who knew him as a boy.
Back at the house the news is a broken ceasefire.
He stumbles past a fireguard, a duplicator,
hunting for bags to throw away the suits.

Lilies

Like fat aunts at weddings and funerals
tossing their heads, lips curled,
lurching to Mahler or Mendelssohn,
showing off, mouths open,
on top tables and coffins
(the beat of a heart against satin,
love you, Mum, farewell) they slide
into oblivion and the last waltz.

Doors

In junk yards and stone basements smelling of caustic
they're layered like heavy pictures in art shops,
falling back on themselves. We're looking for pre-war,
narrow panels, high handles the kids can't reach,
to match the originals replaced (not by us) with glass
which our boys broke in a year, then with cheap plywood.

Now affluent, impatient, we settle on huge four-panelled
that swung a hundred years in an isolated farmhouse,
jointed from solid pine it takes two days to saw to fit.
The grandchildren flit and dive with the phantoms
of father and uncles, slamming or leaving them open,
making draughts till we yell at them to stop.

Mother's Day

for Mark

Roses line the gutter as the rose sellers
go home, card houses fall, hearts melt

in shop windows. The others forget
or consider it unimportant, except you

who sketch me a house, a sun, a flower,
remembering how to draw like a child.

At dusk we stroll by the edge of a wood
spotting the bats. You tell me about your first trip:

swimming roads in slow motion, stepping
through perspex into a trashed city.

Fish

His foot turns as it did in childhood,
though the doctors swore it would right itself,
and his left boot wears on one side.
His spine pays back with a bad neck
which clicks and aches when he overdoes it,
carrying food three miles, or water from the tap.

They're called layabouts, never done a hand's turn;
he's raising three boys, with the same woman
since seventeen. They're horse travellers,
living in the wagon he built, curved top,
a high step you'd sit on to whistle at the world;
inside on frosty mornings a wood stove
boils a kettle in forty minutes.

The kids bundled in layers of castoffs
till they'd roll like cheeses if you pushed them
run redfaced round the verges they've turned in on,
dodging cars as drivers put their foot down.

The Festival Called Holi

Last night I heard a story from a man
who'd been to India and met the Dalai Lama,
who gave him a piece of red string
which he used to fix his new flute;

and I said I thought the Dalai would be pleased
to know his gift had been put to use,
not laid on a shrine and worshipped.
He also told us about the festivals

especially the one called Holi
where people rush round the streets
mixing paint and throwing it at each other.
He still had some in his hair.

Cows wander all over India, as we know,
and, oddly enough, so do the pigs
because they are the opposite of sacred,
but what's the difference between sacred and unclean

if both give you the freedom to bum around
wherever you want and not get eaten?

The Red Road

He travelled up India, took a bus
sixteen hours from Simla to Manali,
last town at the end of the red road
into the foothills – men in grey dhotis
brewing tea in the street: sugar and milk
simmered all day. Two rupees.
Marihuana capital of the world
where everyone speaks English,
the new hotels like slabs of cheese
spoiling the view of the mountains.

Now he's back he wants to tell me about it,
tracing it for me on our large atlas.
I note it down, smiling and nodding –
my family lead such interesting lives,
I write about them, boast to strangers.
He's desperate to tell me it was his thing,
his vision – the dust, the swaying cows,
the heat before the rains came –
but all he's left with is a lump in his throat,
bad guts, a touch of malaria that comes to him
on chilly nights in Kidderminster.

Time

He searches the house for me,
slamming doors, and I'm in my room
writing. He has something to show me,
his story for class, how it will fit
the three minutes he's scheduled for.
He's a stickler, a professional
at thirteen, drafting and redrafting,
reading aloud against the alarm clock,
his life so full of flux and chances,
like a baby he doesn't have to learn
how to. It happens. I harvest time,
harbour it in precious bowls,
this for this, this for that. And this hour
is mine, like good liquor, a bottle
from another country, once drunk, gone forever,
the sort they don't stock down the road.

Patience

It takes time you could be cooking with
or reading books in, an effort,
a push on an armchair,
a hobble. It gets in your eyes,
behind the heart. Stretch muscle and
lift, watch the cat, do what he does:
all day on a duvet
waiting for his dreams to wake him,
go hunting again.
That's the thing about it,
what they told you it would take,
and the limits on keeping going,
doing what they said would improve matters.
And it does so's you wouldn't notice,
movements like a cat's dream,
a breeze across water,
and you're dipping a toe, then wading,
a full splash, and the sea's yours again,
ready to be swum across, dived into,
knowing the evidence is still there.

'Griff'

The barge we've come to look at, maybe buy,
sits wedged in ice on the opposite bank,
low and sturdy. Across the canal Nathan hails us:
'Don't fall in the water, you'll break a leg.'
But it's not strong enough to bear our weight.
We feel our way back along the slippy towpath
to where the ice thins in the shelter of the bridge.

Towards Pendle beyond a field of ponies
the hills are veined with snow. The boatyard's full
of broken hulks: Gemini, Forget-me-not.
From a caravan a man throws slops.
Here people live their peaceful, messy lives
littered with tarps and mud, gas cylinders,
empty flowerpots stacked on cabin roofs.

There's something about living inside wood:
a wagon, a barge, feeling the walls are alive,
their friendly curves and limitations.
Like the business of walking on ice,
of trusting your legs not to crease and fall,
bearing the weight downwards so your knees
don't ache with the strain of a body too heavy for them.

The cabin feels like home. Nathan explains
the engine, the leaks in the bilges.
He likes to travel at night, hoisting the lights,
slipping moorings like a smuggler,
only the diesel's low hum to upset the ducks.
We shake on it. On the little stove a stew
bubbles away, happy with the occasional stir.

Gap Year

A double spoon to measure
sugar and salt, mix with clean water,
a solution to settle a stomach,
        to be 'no saltier than tears'.

Sterile needles, short wave radio,
nine months' supply of classics,
sunblock, clean socks, hat and mac
        for when the rains set in.

Hug the cat. Five hour drive:
holiday queues, cars in a shunt,
hay cart sheds its load,
        police wail on the hard shoulder.

Terminal 3. Africans fly home,
Arabs and Chinese deal on mobiles.
Dash round the bookstall, last snaps
        as he walks down the ramp, slips away

behind the flats, like an actor, waving.
Three days later, a crackling line,
too much to say in seconds
        so we say nothing except goodbye.

Raspberry Jam

I picked them myself the day before,
red stains up to the elbows;
topping and boiling took a whole Morse
(the one where Lewis falls in the Isis).

Anything to welcome him home,
take his mind off things, and mine –
some bits labelled 'Mum don't read this',
but rumours have already reached us:

bush trip complete with lions;
the dawn push to the summit
of Kili, his slip on the ice
down the side of a precipice.

When we meet at Heathrow, him dressed
in scarlet Masai cloak and sandals, it's as if
he's never been gone, and we drive home,
the coming day a red smear the size of Africa.

Tin Roofs

It's more than malaria gets in the blood
in Africa: its red-soiled, potholed towns,
jungles of car parts, sewing machines,
mended T-shirts from Leeds and Seattle,
herdsmen lean as their cows.

We were asked out as honoured guests.
In the village where we stopped on the way
for yams and cooking oil, every other roof
an advert for Omo or Blueband,
an ancestral tableau of gossiping women
gathered by the standpipe with plastic demijohns,
and far from the cities young boys
begged to be photographed.

And if we hadn't turned up when we did
to hoik Emile's father's barrow up
alongside the spare fuel on the LandRover
he'd have strapped it on the next bus up the mountain
squashing someone's mangoes
and their chickens too, probably.

If you catch it you ache in places
you didn't know you had
but the local medics know their stuff,
and not till you're back home,
years later maybe,
does it grip you again, the fever.

On Roosevelt Island

which even New Yorkers don't know about,
the cable rising over the spit of the bridge
across the East River after a long haul up Sixth
and a stop to buy wine though I know you only drink
vodka,
you're five floors up, an exile,
books and piano slippage from the other life,
your own tongue precious as a photograph.

In my country, where we first met, it was winter,
by the sea, and in the bar your voice held audience,
they even applauded.

                There's wood smoke in the air
but nostalgia doesn't count any more,
only loneliness,
                   and now I'm back home,
autumn settling into the valley,
there's no place for it,
nothing to stop it, nothing,
as the day becomes evening and clouds
balance on the hills like heroes, for it.

Once

Tonight it's a blue moon.
Our last day here, end of June,

things are working a treat –
in the Museum of Modern Art

the paint's flaking, raw material
under my fingernails,

onto the carpet off the Rothkos,
the poppy red ones. Photos

in front of the Pollocks,
arms round each other, bikemarks

curling like firework traces.
The print won't fit in our suitcase.

The trees say: don't look at us, we're just trees.
The sky pulls down behind the Chrysler,
and the evening makes itself. The moon rises.

She Thought She'd Found God

but not in the usual places
(heart, mind, body)
nor in the small things:
spiders, milk bottles, dandelions.
There were no messages or signs.
She'd tried everything: aromatherapy,
had been down rabbit holes,
up crystal ladders.
She'd always thought of God
as buttoned up in a dead language,
filling gaps in the teeth of atheists.
She wasn't sure of her discovery
except the air felt different
and she'd begun finding good points
in people she didn't like
(this worried her). But that was it.
She carried on eyeing up the quality,
shouting at her mother,
and God carried on being
more of a question than an answer
and not of her asking.